My First Book
Irish Songs
and
Celtic Dances

21 Favorite Pieces in Easy Piano Arrangements

Bergerac

With Illustrations by
Marty Noble

DOVER PUBLICATIONS, INC.
Mineola, New York

Bibliographical Note

My First Book of Irish Songs and Celtic Dances: 21 Favorite Pieces in Easy Piano Arrangements is a new work, first published by Dover Publications, Inc., in 1998.

International Standard Book Number: 0-486-40405-6

Manufactured in the United States of America
Dover Publications, Inc., 31 East 2nd Street, Mineola, N.Y. 11501

Contents

. . . and, at long last, this special one is for Ryan Calligan, with love

Sure, and it's said that on Saint Paddy's Day, all the world is Irish! No matter our roots, we tap our feet to those rollicking Irish reels . . . feel patriots' fever at the sound of Celtic pipes and drums . . . shed a light tear for those long-lost loves from Erin and Tralee . . . and wonder—along with everyone else—who *really* put the overalls in Mistress Murphey's chowder!

Have fun with these gems from the Emerald Isle!

O'Bergerac

Who Threw the Overalls in Mistress Murphey's Chowder?

Words & music: George L. Geifer (1898)

Bright and saucy

Who threw the o-ver-alls in Mis-tress Mur-phy's chow-der?

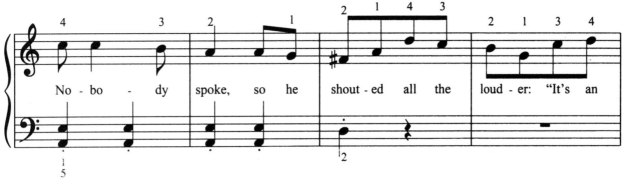

No-bo-dy spoke, so he shout-ed all the loud-er: "It's an

I - rish trick, that's true, I can lick the mick that threw the

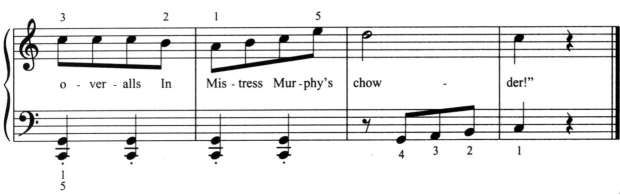

o - ver-alls In Mis-tress Mur-phy's chow - der!"

The Irish Washerwoman

Traditional reel (18th c.)

Bright and light!

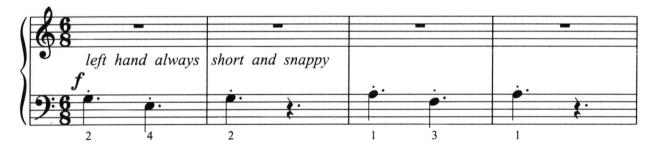

8

1st time: Light and airy / *2nd time:* Forceful and lively!

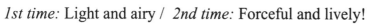

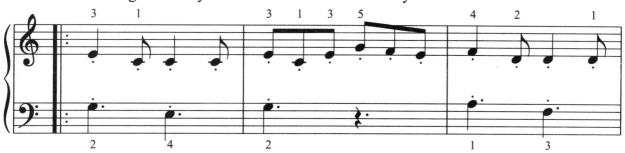

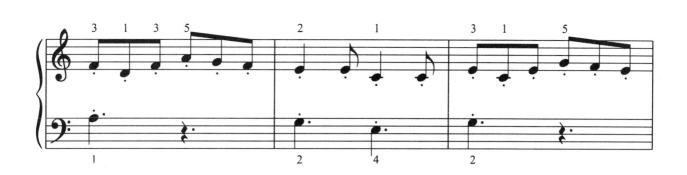

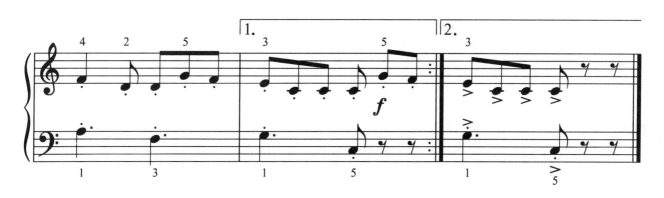

Molly Malone
("Cockles 'n' Mussels")

Quietly, telling a story

Anonymous ballad

In Dub - lin fair ci - ty, _____ where girls are so pret - ty, _____ 'Twas _____ there I first met with sweet Mol - ly Ma - lone. She drove a wheel - bar - row _____ 'thro streets broad and

10

nar - row, ___ Cry - ing "Cock - les 'n' mus - sels, a -

Very slow (the end of the story)

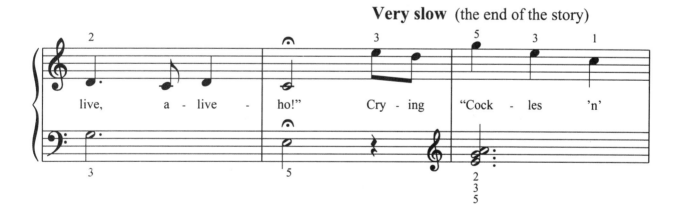

live, a - live - ho!" Cry - ing "Cock - les 'n'

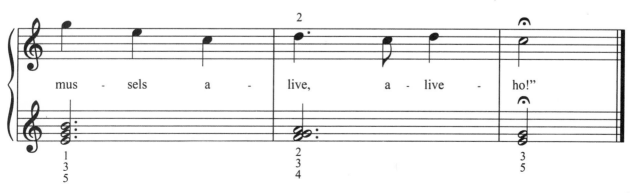

mus - sels a - live, a - live - ho!"

The Wearing of the Green

Words: Dion Boucicault

Music: Anon. (ca. 1845)

Sound the horns!

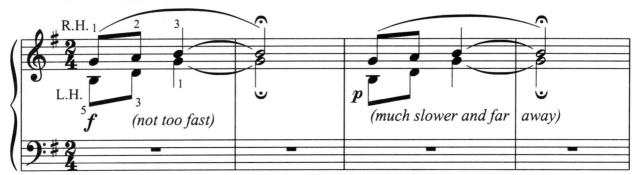

(not too fast) *(much slower and far away)*

Sound the drums! A bright march!

Oh! —

Vigorous and strong

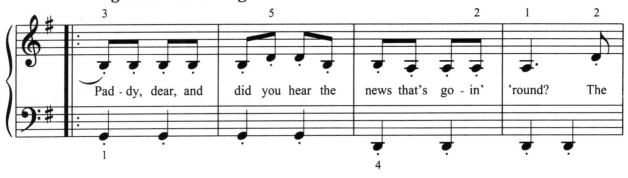

Pad - dy, dear, and did you hear the news that's go - in' 'round? The

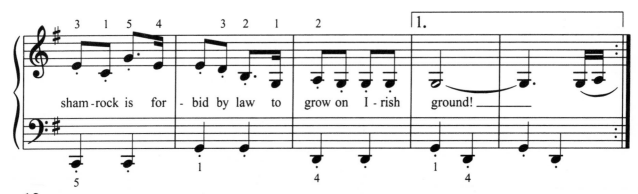

sham-rock is for - bid by law to grow on I - rish ground! —

Oh! Paddy, dear, and did you hear the news that's goin' 'round?
The shamrock is forbid by law to grow on Irish ground!
Saint Patrick's Day no more we'll keep, his color can't be seen,
For there's a bitter law agin' the Wearin' o' the Green.

Celtic Drums and Pipes

Traditional

A powerful march, very steady

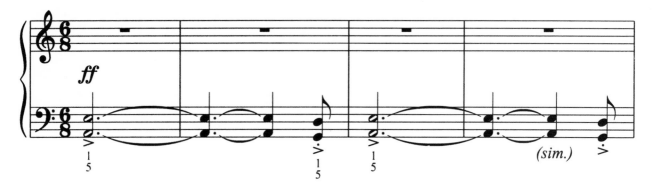

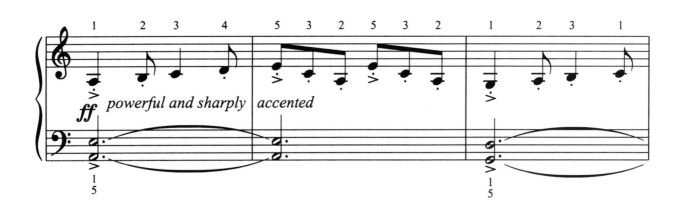

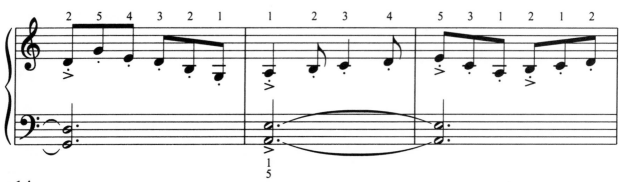

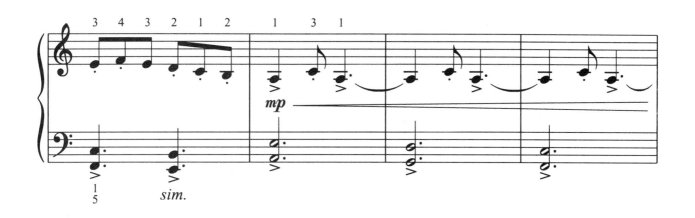

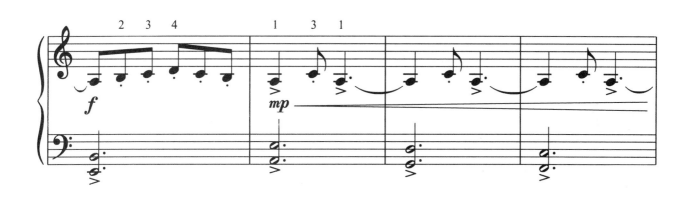

(Keep the beat even as you get softer!)

Maid Colleen

Based on "Collen dhas cruthen na moe,"
an anonymous Irish ballad (18th c.)

Slowly flowing

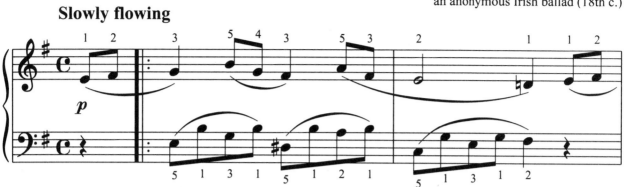

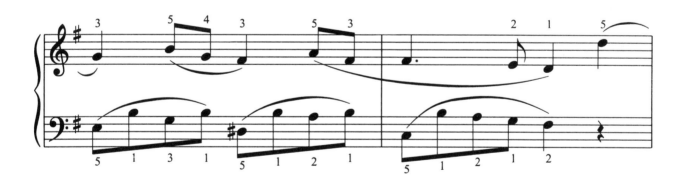

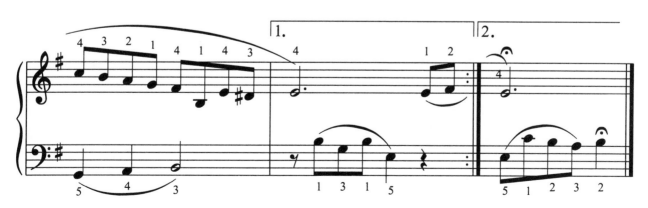

Danny Boy

Words: Frederick E. Weatherly (1913)

Music: "Londonderry Air" (anonymous)

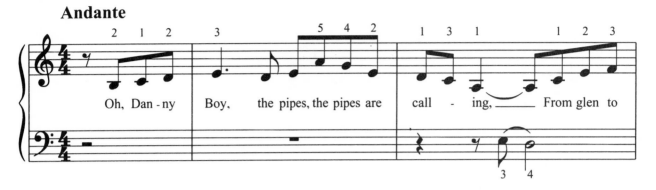

Oh, Dan-ny Boy, the pipes, the pipes are call - ing, ___ From glen to

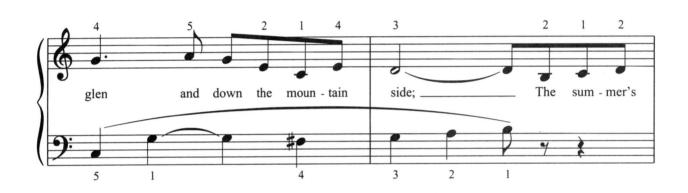

glen and down the moun-tain side; ___ The sum-mer's

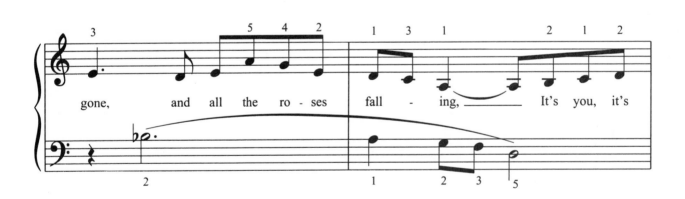

gone, and all the ro-ses fall - ing, ___ It's you, it's

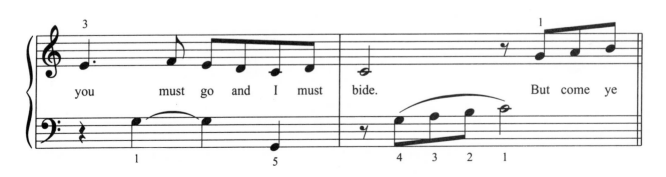

you must go and I must bide. But come ye

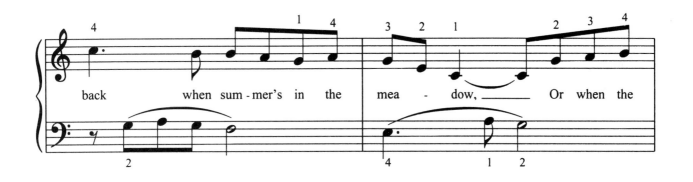

back   when sum-mer's in the   mea - dow, _____ Or when the

val -   ley's hushed and white with   snow, _____ _____ It's I'll be

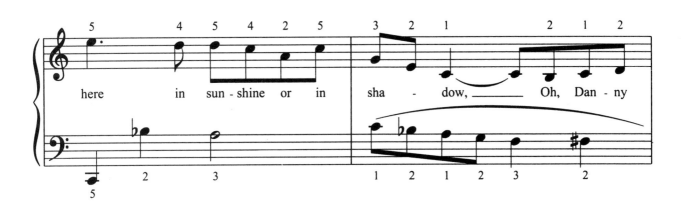

here   in sun-shine or in   sha - dow, _____ Oh, Dan - ny

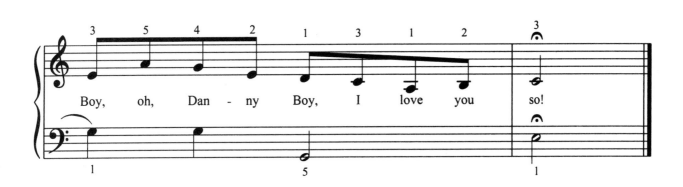

Boy,   oh,   Dan - ny   Boy,   I   love   you   so!

19

The Kerry Dance

Words: J. L. Molloy (1879)

Music: Based in part on Margaret Casson's "The Cuckoo" (1790)

A lively 2-beat dance

O the days of the Ker - ry danc - ing,

O the ring of the pi - per's tune!

O for one of those hours of glad - ness,

Gone, a - las! like our youth, too soon:

Freely (slow down!) *(wait)* *(wait)*

mp O to think of it, O to dream of it,

fills my heart with tears!

Fast Again!

O the days of the Ker - ry danc - ing,

O the ring of the pi - per's tune!

Sweet Rosie O'Grady

Words & music: Maude Nugent (1896)

Light and tinkly - like a quiet music box

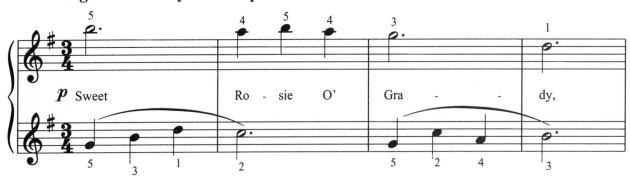

p Sweet Ro - sie O' Gra - - dy,

My dear lit - tle Rose, ____

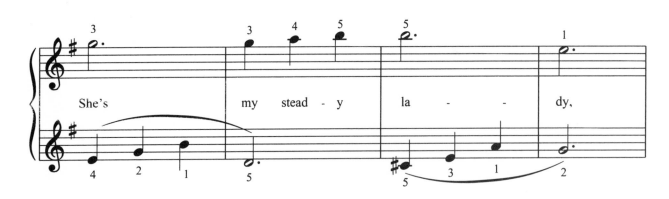

She's my stead - y la - - dy,

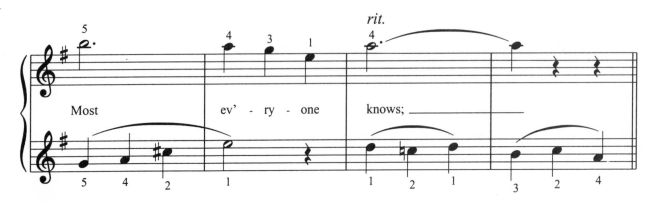

Most ev' - ry - one knows; ____

rit.

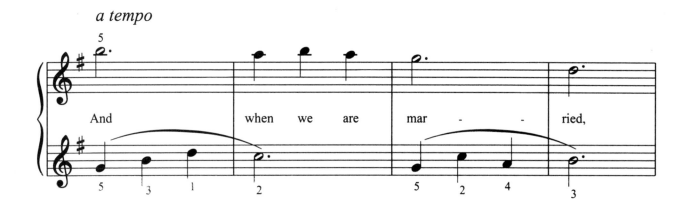

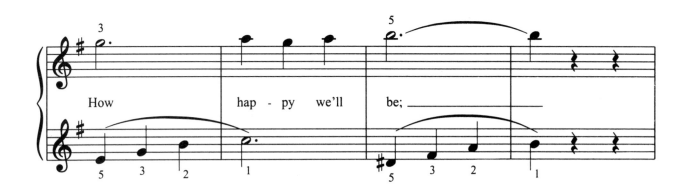

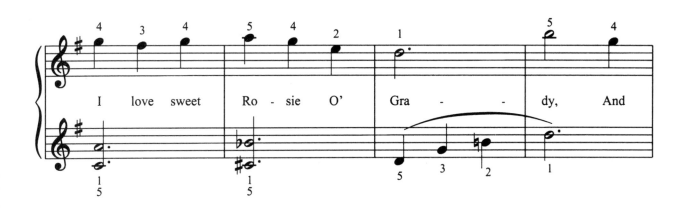

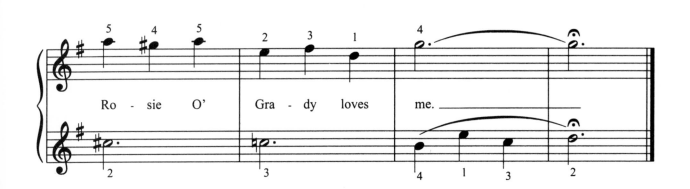

Native Swords
(Irish Patriot's Song)

Words & Music: Thomas David (1896)

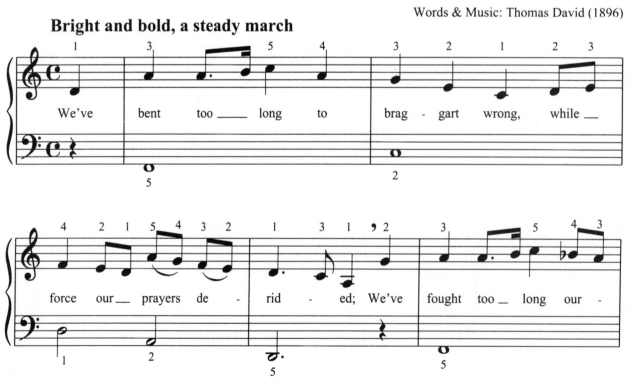

Bright and bold, a steady march

We've bent too ___ long to brag - gart wrong, while ___ force our ___ prayers de - rid - ed; We've fought too ___ long our -

selves a - mong, by ___ knaves and ___ clans ___ di - vi - ded. U -

a little quieter, less forceful

nit - ed ___ now, no more we'll bow, Foul fac - tion ___ we ___ dis -

gradually bigger and bolder -

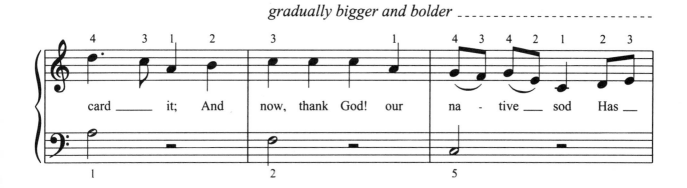

card ___ it; And now, thank God! our na - tive ___ sod Has ___

- - - - - - - - - - *gradually slower, more forceful*

na - tive ___ swords ___ to ___ guard it.

25

Too-Ra-Loo-Ra-Loo-Ral
(That's an Irish Lullaby)

Words & music: James R. Shannon (1913)

Easy-going, restrained

"Too - ra - loo - ra - loo - ral, ___

Too - ra - loo - ra - li, ___

Too - ra - loo - loo - ral, ___

Hush, now, don't you cry! ___

Too - ra - loo - ra - loo - ral, _____

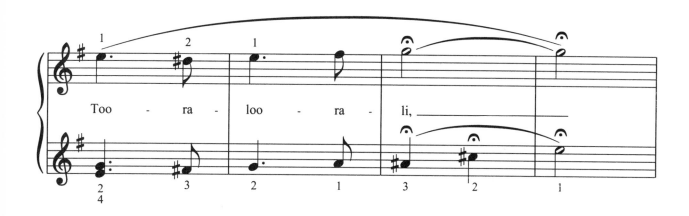

Too - ra - loo - ra - li, _____

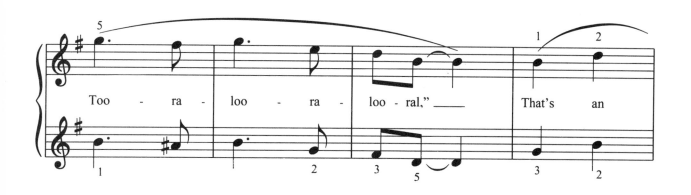

Too - ra - loo - ra - loo - ral," _____ That's an

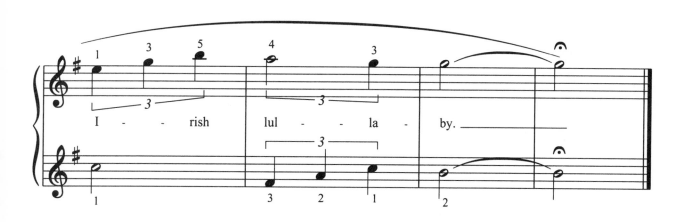

I - - rish lul - la - by. _____

The Rose of Tralee

Words: C. Mordaunt Spencer

Music: Charles W. Glover (ca. 1845)

A lilting, gentle waltz

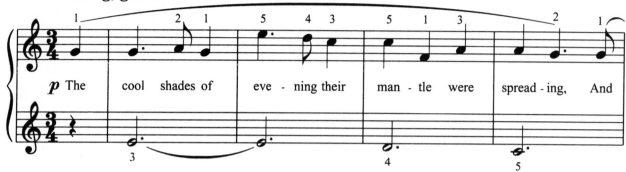

p The cool shades of eve - ning their man - tle were spread - ing, And

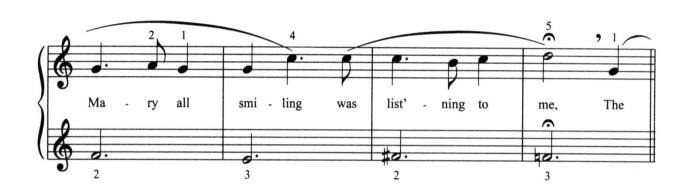

Ma - ry all smi - ling was list' - ning to me, The

moon thro' the val - ley her pale rays was shed - ding, When

I won the heart of the Rose of Tra - lee.

When Irish Eyes Are Smiling

Words: Chauncey Alcott & George Graff Jr.

Music: Ernest R. Ball (1912)

A waltz with a nice swing to it

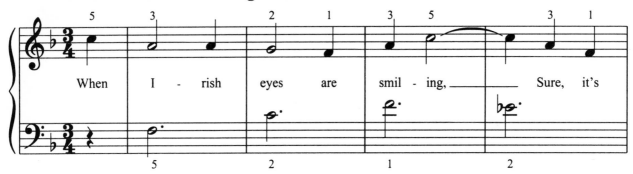

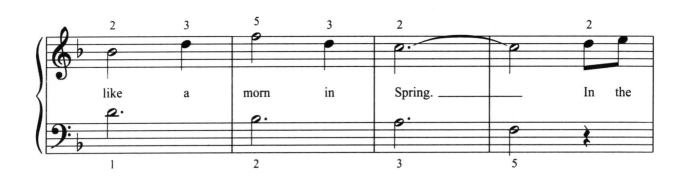

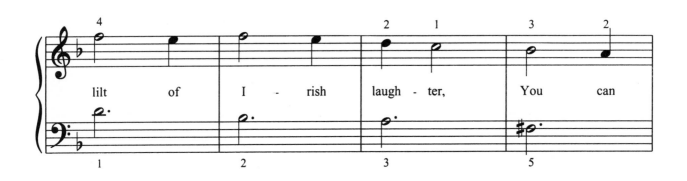

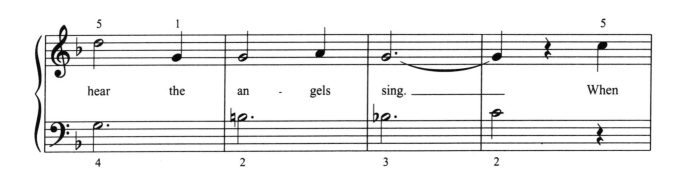

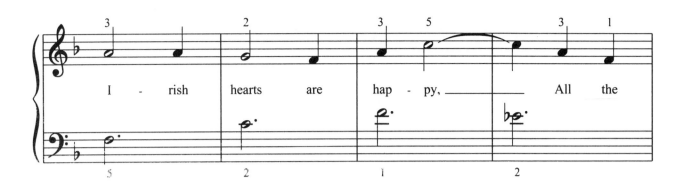

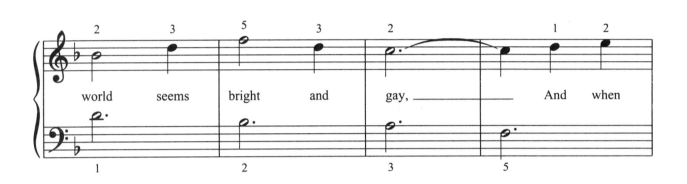

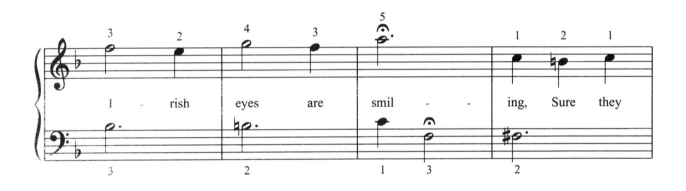

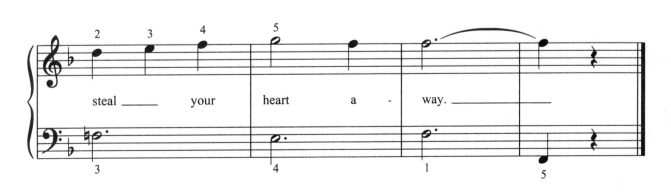

The Mulligan Band

Based on an interlude from "The Mulligan Guard"
by Ned Harrigan and David Braham (1873)

With a strong beat, but not too fast

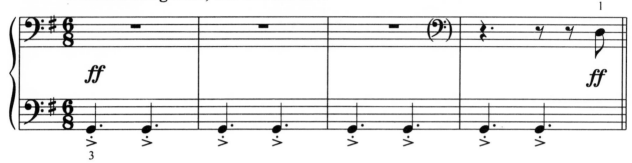

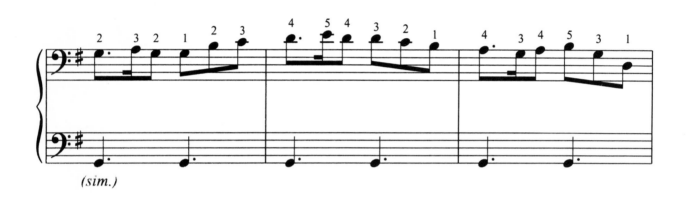

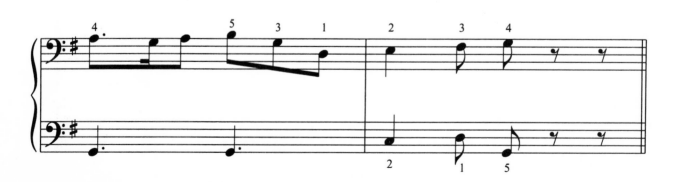

(The band marches off, gradually going farther and farther away.)

(slightly held back)

(even more held back as the band disappears . . .)

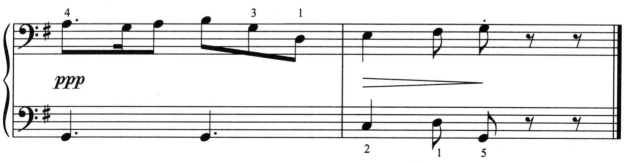

The Minstrel-Boy

Words: Thomas Moore (1813)

Music: "Moreen" (?) (anonymous)

A march in moderate tempo

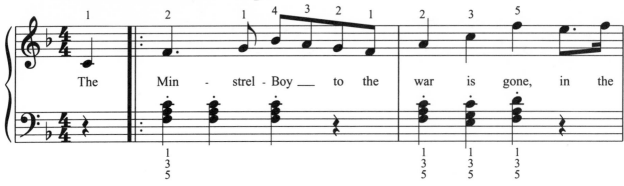

The Min - strel - Boy ___ to the war is gone, in the

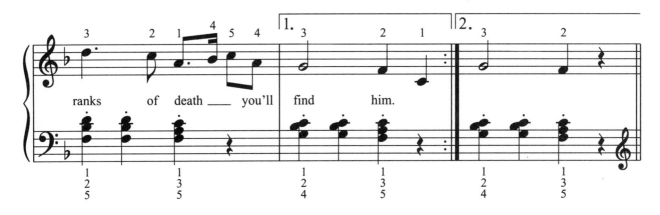

ranks of death ___ you'll find him.

Much slower- quiet and sad

"Land of Song," said the War - rior Bard, "Tho' all the world be -

March tempo

trays ___ thee, One sword at least ___ thy ___ Right shall guard, One ___

Slowly, quietly, reflectively

faith - ful harp ___ shall praise thee. *p legato*

35

My Wild Irish Rose

Words & music: Chauncey Olcott (1899)

Very gently and restrained

where, but none can com - pare, With my

rall. *a tempo*

1.

wild I - rish Rose.

2.

wild ___ I - - rish Rose. ___

When Johnny Comes Marching Home

By "Louis Lambert" (Patrick S. Gilmore),
probably based on a 19th-century ballad

Moving along at a good pace

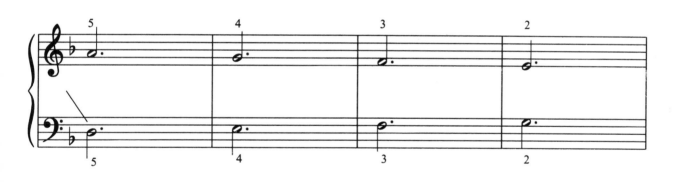

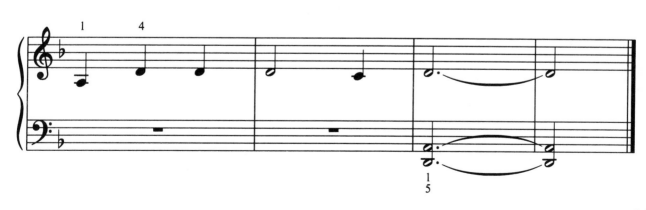

39

Drill, Ye Tarriers, Drill!

A fantasy on music possibly composed
by Thomas Casey (1888)

Forceful, driving hard

Come Back to Erin

Words & music: "Claribel" (Charlotte Barnard) (1866)

Gently flowing

Come back to E - rin, Ma - vour - neen, Ma - vour - neen;

Come back, A - roon, to the land of my birth;

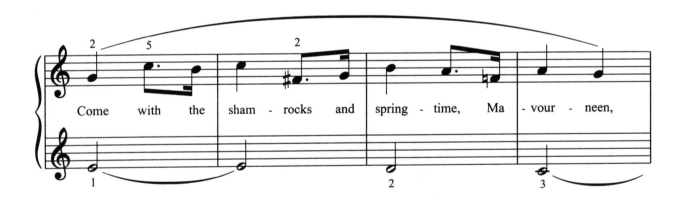

Come with the sham - rocks and spring - time, Ma - vour - neen,

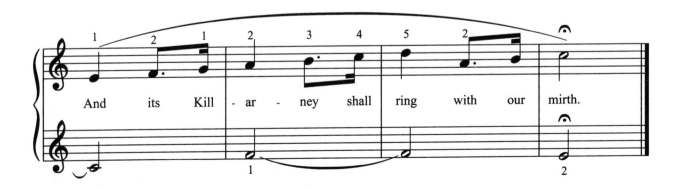

And its Kill - ar - ney shall ring with our mirth.

The Pipers of Feagh MacHugh
("Follow Me Up to Carlow")

Battle song (ca. 1580)

(slight ritard)

Full force!

ff *(Feagh MacHugh | attacks Carlow)*

Slow and heavy!

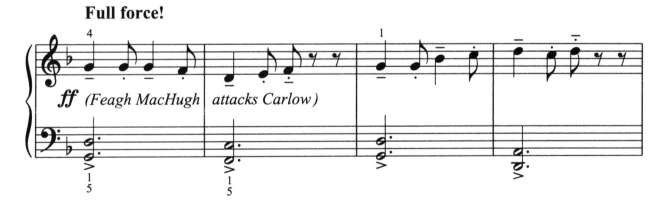

fff

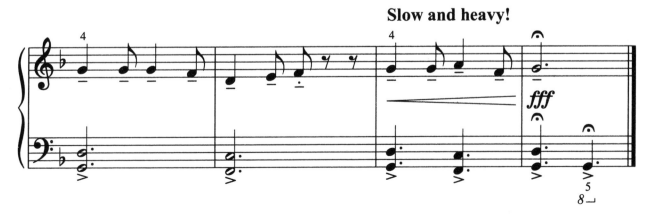

45

Rulla Rulla
(Ancient Celtic Reel)

Lively, with robust good feeling

1st time: ***f*** */ 2nd time:* ***p***

1st time: ***f*** */ 2nd time:* ***p***

Repeat the whole dance as many times as you like!
But for the very last time, slow down the final four bars.